THE WORLD'S MOST AMAZING
ANIMAL FACTS
For Kids

First published in Great Britain in 2002 by
Dean, an imprint of Egmont Books Limited,
239 Kensington High Street,
London W8 6SA

Copyright © 2002 Egmont Books Limited

ISBN 0 603 56060 1

1 3 5 7 9 10 8 6 4 2

Printed and bound in the U.A.E.

THE WORLD'S MOST AMAZING
ANIMAL FACTS
For Kids

Regans
Book of
Facts

Written and Compiled by: Guy Campbell & Mark Devins
Illustrated by: Paul Moran & Simon Ecob

The first living creature to orbit the earth was a Husky dog called Laika, sent into space by Russia in 1957 aboard Sputnik II.

Chickens are among the bird world's most embarrassingly poor aviators. The longest recorded flight of a chicken is thirteen seconds.

Dogs were probably the first animals ever to be domesticated by man. The dogs would warn their human friends of approaching danger, and lead hunters to sources of food.

The largest fish in the world is the Whale Shark, which grows to more than 50 feet in length and can weigh several tons.

Tarantulas do not use muscles to move their legs. They walk by controlling the amount of blood they pump into their legs to make them longer and shorter.

The waters around Australia are home to more than half of all the shark species in the world.

More animals are killed by motorists than by hunters with guns.

Elephants and humans are the only animals that can do headstands.

A cat has 32 muscles in each ear.

A cockroach can live for up to nine days without its head, before it starves to death.

Eggs that are laid in nests are usually plain white. Eggs laid on the ground are speckled so that they look like the ground around them and are hard to see.

The Poison-arrow Frog contains enough deadly poison to kill about 2,200 people.

Male monkeys go bald in the same way that human men do.

Sharks never get sick: they are immune to all known diseases, including cancer.

Contrary to the phrase "sweating like a pig", pigs can't actually sweat.

African Elephants have only four teeth to chew their food with.

A house fly lives for only 14 days.

Lobsters can regenerate some of their body parts. For example: the claws, legs, and antennae. If they need to, they can shed a claw or a leg that another creature has grabbed, and grow another one later.

Most cows give more milk when they listen to music.

25% of cat owners blow-dry their cat's hair after a bath.

Kangaroos usually have one young annually. The young kangaroo, or joey, is born alive at a very immature stage, when it is only about 2cm long and weighs less than a gram.

Emus lay emerald green eggs.

Roosters can't crow if they can't fully extend their necks.

The underside of a horse's hoof is called a frog. The frog peels off several times a year with new growth.

The placement of a donkey's eyes in its head enables it to see all four feet at all times.

A duck's quack doesn't echo, and no-one knows why.

Kiwis live in pairs and mate for life (sometimes as long as 30 years).

The Mola Mola, or Ocean Sunfish, lays up to five million eggs at one time.

A fully grown bear can run as fast as a horse.

The Sumatran Tiger has the most stripes of all the tigers. The Siberian Tiger is the least stripy.

The Honey Badger can withstand hundreds of African Bee stings that would kill any other animal.

More human deaths have been attributed to fleas than all the wars ever fought. As carriers of the bubonic plague, fleas were responsible for killing one third of the population of Europe in the 14th century.

The only purple animal is the South African Blesbok.

The Blue Whale is probably the largest animal ever to inhabit the Earth. Examples have been measured at 31 metres (100 feet) in length - roughly the length of a basketball court.

Orangutans warn other creatures to stay out of their territory by belching loudly.

Research indicates that mosquitoes are particularly attracted to people who have recently eaten bananas.

Slugs have four noses.

The average garden variety caterpillar has 248 muscles in its head.

The average porcupine has more than 30,000 quills.

A lot of sea creatures make something like a pearl, but the real pearl-producing oysters are found only in the waters of the Indo-Pacific.

Although most species of dog eat meat, they are also partial to fruit.

Contrary to popular opinion, wolves hardly ever bite humans.

Grasshoppers have learned to "hear" with their legs, waving them in the air like little TV aerials feeling for sound waves.

An annoyed camel will spit at a person.

Cats have five toes on each front paw, but only four toes on each back paw.

Beavers can hold their breath for <u>45 minutes</u>.

An Earthworm has five hearts.

A hedgehog's heart beats about 300 times in a minute.

The Three-Toed Sloth is the slowest animal in the world. It can take several days for it to climb a medium–sized tree.

Scientists in Siberia recently located a woolly mammoth carcass. They removed the carcass from the frozen tundra and transported it to an ice cellar in Khatanga, Russia. The mammoth died at the age of 47 about 20,000 years ago. Plans are in place to attempt cloning of the mammoth by transplanting a cell nucleus into an elephant egg, and implanting it into a living elephant to make a baby mammoth.

The woolly mammoth, extinct since the last Ice Age, had tusks almost 16 feet long.

Toads don't have teeth. Frogs do.

A lion's roar can be heard from over five miles away.

Emus cannot walk backwards. Neither can Kangaroos.

A dolphin's hearing is so acute that it can pick up an underwater sound from 15 miles away.

During the Second World War, British Prime Minister Winston Churchill kept a Poodle called Rufus. German leader Adolf Hitler had an Alsatian called Blondi.

There are more beetles than any other kind of creature in the world.

Did you know...

...that of all the animals in the world, bats have the most sensitive hearing?

There is a type of parrot in New Zealand, called a Kea, that likes to eat the rubber strips that line car windows.

The clock on Big Ben was made to lose time when a passing group of migrating starlings decided to take a breather on the minute hand.

A Polar Bear's fur is not white, it's colourless.

Polar Bears' skin is actually black. Their hairs are hollow and act like fiberoptics, directing sunlight to warm their skin.

Polar Bears camouflage themselves more completely during a hunt by covering their black noses with their paws.

It takes 3,000 cows to supply the National Football League with enough leather for a year's supply of footballs.

Ostrich skeletons and fossils have been found which date back over 120 million years - Ostriches are a true "dinosaur".

A chimpanzee can learn to recognize itself in a mirror, but monkeys can't.

A cow can give about 200,000 glasses of milk in her lifetime.

A woodpecker can peck 20 times a second.

The food company Ben and Jerry's send the waste from making ice cream to local pig farmers to use as feed. The pigs love all flavours of ice cream except Mint Oreo.

Rudolph, the Red-Nosed Reindeer, was invented in 1939, in Chicago, for the Montgomery Ward department store's Christmas promotion.

In 1925, the most popular movie star in America, as voted by cinemagoers, was a dog. Rin Tin Tin made over 40 films, earned more than a million dollars and received 10,000 fan letters a week!

The teeth of a lobster are in its stomach.

An ant can lift things ten times its own weight.

A giraffe has exactly the same number of bones in its neck as a mouse does.

A butterfly warms up its body to 81 degrees Fahrenheit before flying.

The tongue of a Blue Whale is about the same size as an elephant.

A giraffe can clean its ears with its 50cm (20 in) tongue.

Cats don't always kill for food. Often they kill something and bring it to their owners as a gift. So if you see a dead animal on the doorstep, don't be angry, praise your cat. It's a sign of affection!

A snail has two pairs of tentacles on its head. One pair is longer than the other and houses the eyes. The shorter pair is used for smelling and feeling its way around.

Bees are fully grown when they are born.

A scallop has a total of 35 eyes which are all blue.

An estimated 80% of animals on Earth have six legs.

Mongooses were brought to Hawaii to kill rats. The plan failed because rats go out at night and mongooses hunt in the day.

33 per cent of American dog owners admit that they talk to their dogs on the phone or leave messages on the answering machine when they are away.

The Museum of Natural History named a spider, Calponia Harrisonfordi, after actor Harrison Ford.

All elephants walk on tiptoe, because the back portion of their foot is made up of fat and has no bone.

Cats cannot taste sweets.

Dalmatian dogs originate from the Dalmatian coast of Croatia.

The hippopotamus has skin an inch and a half thick, so solid that most bullets cannot go through it.

A blind chameleon will still change colour to match his environment.

Some Australian earthworms grow up to ten feet long.

The largest carnivorous mammal ever found was an 11-foot-tall polar bear.

The giraffe is the only animal on earth that is born with horns on the forehead in both genders.

A pregnant goldfish is called a twit.

During WWII, Americans tried to train bats to drop bombs.

Rats like boiled sweets better than they like cheese.

Murphy's Oil Soap is the most popular for cleaning elephants.

When a female horse and male donkey mate, the baby is called a mule, but when a male horse and female donkey mate, the baby is called a hinny.

The cleverest breeds of dog are, in order:
1) **Border Collie**
2) **Poodle**
3) **Golden Retriever**

The Afghan Hound is one of the stupidest.

The Ostrich is the second fastest animal in the world and can run at 40 miles per hour. They can also keep this speed up for at least 30 minutes.

A bear has 42 teeth.

Besides special eyes and ears, owls have special feathers. The flight feathers are soft and fluffy and have fuzzy edges, so there is no swishing sound when the bird flies through the air. Most of the little creatures an owl catches never hear it coming.

George Washington's favourite horse was named Lexington. Napoleon Bonaparte's favourite was called Marengo.

The Anabas Fish from Southern Asia has special oxygen-absorbing gills that allow it to leave the water and walk on land. It has even been known to climb trees.

If birds went into space they would soon die. They need gravity to swallow.

Crows have the biggest brains, relative to body size, of any bird.

Most snakes have only one lung.

The pet ferret was domesticated more than 500 years before the cat.

The cat is the only domestic animal not mentioned in the Bible.

A zebra is white with black stripes.

There is a sea squirt found in the seas near Japan that digests its own brain. When the sea squirt is mature, it permanently attaches itself to a rock. At this point it does not need to move any more and has no need for a brain. So it eats it.

Which came first, the chicken or the egg?
According to the Bible (Genesis 1:20-22),
it was the chicken.

An animal epidemic is called an epizootic.

The word "Amphibious" comes from the
Greek for "living a double life". Amphibious
animals live both on land and in water.

**The phrase "Happy as a clam" comes
from "Happy as a clam at high tide."
Clams are harvested when the tide is out.**

There are over ten million horses in China.

**If a Turkey Vulture is disturbed
or harassed, it will throw up on whoever
or whatever is bothering it.**

Horses expend more energy lying down
than they do when they are standing up.

The world's scariest fish has to be the Pirhana. It is quite small with vicious-looking teeth and will attack anything that moves. In 1981, a boat carrying 300 people sank in the port of Obidos in Brazil. A passing shoal of Pirhanas couldn't believe their luck, and ate every last person.

Polar bears have been tracked swimming continuously for up to 62 miles.

Did you know...

...that to stay in the air, bees must flap their wings two hundred and fifty times every second?

Towser, a tortoise-shell cat in charge of rodent control in Glen Turret Distillery, Fife, Scotland, killed 28,899 mice in her 21 years. This is about four mice per day, every day, for 21 years.

Only pregnant female polar bears hibernate.

The beaver has special valves that keep water out of its ears.

A seagull can drink seawater because it has special glands that filter out the salt.

Snoopy was based on Spike, the beagle owned by cartoonist Charles Schulz. Nana from 'Peter Pan' was originally Luath, the big shaggy Newfoundland dog owned by writer J.M. Barrie.

An elephant trunk has no bone, but 40,000 muscles.

Collections of animals have been given some strange names in the English language. We correctly refer to: a pride of lions, leap of leopards, sloth of bears, knot of toads, bouquet of pheasants, troop of kangaroos, mustering of storks, gang of elk, clouter of cats, kindle of kittens, pack of dogs, leash of greyhounds, trip of goats, root of wolves, adrift of hogs, parliament of owls, tiding of magpies, siege of herons, peep of chickens, exaltation of larks, murder of crows, unkindness of ravens, ostentation of peacocks, skulk of foxes, shrewdness of apes, and a crash of rhinos!

A large feather is made up of over a million different fibres, barbs and hooks.

You might have a goldfish yourself at home, but the king of pet fish has to be the Japanese Koi. These beautiful and very valuable creatures grace posh ponds all over the world. In 1982, a champion Koi was sold for a record £50,000. Unfortunately for the new owner, it died just a few months later.

A Blue Whale weighs the same as about 30 elephants.

The Hummingbird is the only bird that can fly backwards.

A Dung Beetle will spend ages rolling a little ball of dung about until it finds a little hole to put it in. Then it lays its eggs in it and waits for the kids to hatch.

The Monarch Butterfly likes to get around. One of the little flappers was tracked from Ontario in Canada to Angangueo in Mexico, a distance of 3,432 km (2,133 miles).

Goats' and octopuses' eyes have rectangular pupils.

Fish that live more than 800 metres below the ocean surface don't have eyes. It's so dark, there's no point.

The oldest breed of dog is the Saluki.

Ostriches don't bury their heads in the sand.

The South American Giant Anteater eats more than 30,000 ants a day.

It is impossible to out-swim a shark - sharks reach speeds of 70 kph (44 mph). Humans can swim at only about 5 kph (3.1 mph).

There are 701 types of pure-breed dogs.

The Blue-ringed Octopus starts life the size of a pea and is fully grown at about the size of a golf ball - but carries enough poison to kill 26 adults within minutes.

Ants can live up to 16 years.

The elephant is the only animal with four knees, one in each leg.

A large majority of white cats with blue eyes are deaf. White cats with only one blue eye are deaf only in the ear closest to the blue eye. White cats with orange eyes can see and hear just fine.

Nose prints can be used to identify dogs, just as fingerprints can be used to identify humans.

A group of frogs is called an army.

It is possible to lead a cow upstairs but not downstairs, because a cow's knees can't bend properly to walk back down.

Only birds have wishbones.

Flamingos can eat only when their heads are upside down.

Frogs drink and breathe through their skin.

Mountain goats are not really goats. They are antelopes.

Seals can get seasick when they are aboard ships.

Gorillas beat their chests when they get nervous.

Grasshoppers have white blood.

To keep from being separated while sleeping, Sea Otters tie themselves together with seaweed, often drifting miles out to sea during the night.

Studies show that if a cat falls off the seventh floor of a building, it has about a 30 per cent less chance of surviving than a cat that falls off the twentieth floor. It supposedly takes about eight floors for the cat to realise what is occuring, relax and correct itself. At about that height it hits maximum speed and when it hits the ground its rib cage absorbs most of the impact.

A group of geese on the ground is called a gaggle, but a group of geese in the air is called a skein.

The heart of a Blue Whale is the size of a small car.

An ant's sense of smell is as good as a dog's.

You can cut up a starfish into pieces and each piece will grow into a completely new starfish.

A female kangaroo is called a Flyer, and a male is called a Boomer.

Camels have three eyelids to protect themselves from blowing sand.

All the pet hamsters in the world are descended from just one female wild golden hamster found with a litter of twelve young in Syria in 1930.

The embryos of Tiger Sharks fight each other while in their mother's womb, the survivor being the baby shark that is born.

Mother cats teach their kittens to use the litter tray.

An African Elephant cannot be domesticated, but an Indian Elephant can.

The most unsuccessful animal rescue ever took place on January 14, 1978, when volunteers from the British army - filling in for striking firemen - were called by an elderly lady in South London to get her cat out of a tree. They got the cat down with no difficulty whatsoever, and then ran over it as they drove back to the fire station.

The Cheetah is the only cat in the world that can't retract its claws.

Did you know...

...that a female Black Widow Spider can eat up to 20 husbands every day?

Bats are the only mammals that can fly.

Bees have five eyes. There are three small eyes on the top of a bee's head and two larger ones in front.

In 1859, 24 rabbits were released in Australia. Within six years the population had grown to two million.

It takes about four hours to hard-boil an ostrich egg.

Yak's milk is pink.

The hippopotamus is the biggest member of the pig family.

The Archer Fish from Thailand catches its lunch by shooting pellets of water. It has been known to drown a cockroach at a distance of one and a half metres.

Chocolate can be dangerous for dogs. Chocolate affects a dog's heart and nervous system; a few ounces could even be enough to kill a small-sized dog.

The deadly Australian Sea Wasp is the most venomous jellyfish in the world. Its venom has caused the deaths of 66 people off the coast of Queensland since 1880, with victims dying within one to three minutes if medical aid is not available.

All the swans in England are property of the Queen.

Alligators cannot move backwards.

An iguana can stay under water for up to 28 minutes.

Bulls are colour-blind and will charge at a waved cape regardless of its colour.

One of the rarest fish on Earth is the Devil's Hole Pupfish. There may only be 200 of them left, and all the known examples live in the same pond in Nevada, USA.

"Zorro" means "fox" in Spanish.

Of the eight species of tiger known, three of them, the Caspian, Javan and Bali Tigers, have become extinct in the last hundred years. The rarest cat species today is the Indian Lion, with under 200 left in the world, mostly in the Gir National Park in Gujarat, India.

There are a thousand times more living things in the sea than there are on land.

Honey Bees cannot pull their stingers from human skins, and will eventually tear themselves away leaving them behind, causing them to die soon afterwards.

A Crocodile cannot stick its tongue out.

For every person on Earth, there are 200 million insects.

The 20 million Mexican Free-tailed Bats, from the Bracken Cave in Texas, eat 250 tons of insects every night.

When we think of storing up acorns we think of squirrels, but woodpeckers do it too. Woodpeckers drill holes in the sides of trees and pack an acorn into each one. This provides food for the winter when insects are harder to find. A giant pine tree was once discovered with over 50,000 acorns embedded in it.

A polar bear's nostrils close when under water.

The blood of mammals is red, the blood of insects is yellow, and the blood of lobsters is blue.

In England, tunnels have been dug under motorways to enable hedghogs to get across the road without being squashed.

The fastest fish in the world is the Cosmopolitan Sailfish. In Florida, a Sailfish caught on a hook took out 91 metres of fishing line in 3 seconds. This clocks the nippy splosher at around 109 kph.

You are more likely to be killed by a champagne cork than by a poisonous spider.

The most dangerous cat ever was nicknamed the Campawat Man-Eater. It was a tiger that was eventually shot by a naturalist called Jim Corbett, but not before it had eaten over 400 people.

The Stonefish of the tropical Pacific Ocean is so poisonous, one touch from the spines on its fins could kill a man.

A sardine isn't a particular breed of fish. The name has come to mean any small herring-like ocean fish.

Why is fishing sometimes called angling? Because you use a hook, or "angle", to catch the fish (as opposed to a net or your hands).

The stings of ants, bees and wasps are used to inject poison in defence or to paralyse prey. More than 50 different chemicals have been identified from various species.

Fish named after animals include: alligator, bird, boar, buffalo, cat, cow, dog, eagle, elephant, frog, goat, goose, hawk, hog, horse, leopard, lizard, parrot, porcupine, rabbit, sheep, pig, robin, raven, squirrel, tiger, toad, unicorn, viper, wolf, scorpion and zebra.

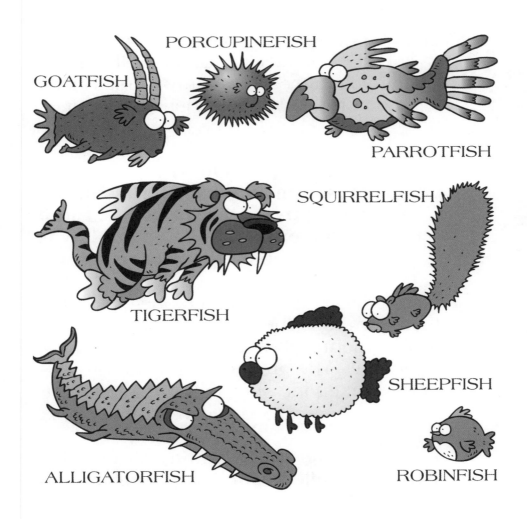

GOATFISH

PORCUPINEFISH

PARROTFISH

TIGERFISH

SQUIRRELFISH

ALLIGATORFISH

SHEEPFISH

ROBINFISH

The most dangerous sharks are (in order of number of attacks): Great White Shark, Bull Shark, Tiger Shark, Grey Nurse Shark, Lemon Shark, Blue Shark, Sand Tiger, Hammerhead and Mako.

The salmon loves to travel, covering thousands of miles of dangerous ocean and raging rivers during its life. But it returns to the exact stream where it was born in order to spawn.

Lobsters come in many colours, but all of them turn red when they are cooked. The red pigment is the most stable colour in a lobster shell. The greens, blues and browns which darken the shell in a live lobster are destroyed by cooking.

Blue Whales feed on tiny shrimp-like crustaceans called Krill. They consume up to eight tons of these animals every day.

Pearls begin with the presence of a foreign body, such as a grain of sand, that lodges in a shell and annoys the oyster inside. The oyster's body reacts by depositing layers of material around the grain to cover it and reduce irritation. In time the little grain of sand thus grows into a pearl.

The largest jellyfish ever caught measured 2.3 m (7 ft 6 ins) across the bell with a tentacle of 36 m (120 ft) long.

Did you know...

...that Oysters change their sex several times during their lives?

A baby Platypus remains blind after birth for eleven weeks.

A chameleon's tongue is twice the length of its body.

A crocodile's tongue is attached to the roof of its mouth.

A large swarm of locusts can eat 80,000 tons of corn in one day.

A rat can last longer without water than a camel can.

A rhinoceros's horn is made of compacted hair.

If your cat is 3 years old, it is about 21 in human years. At the age of 8, it is about 40 in human years. If your cat reaches 14, it is about 70 in human years.

Ants can't chew, they move their jaws sidewards, like a pair of scissors, to extract the juices from the food.

Bees do not have ears.

Cows poo on average 16 times a day.

Elephants have been found swimming miles from the shore in the Indian Ocean.

A dog's nose is so sensitive that it can tell the difference between a bath of water and a bath of water with a teaspoonful of salt in it.

The hippopotamus gives birth underwater.

Pigs almost always sleep on their right side.

The male Howler Monkey of Central and South America is so noisy that it can be heard clearly for distances of up to 3 miles.

A falling cat will always right itself in a precise order. First the head will rotate, then the spine will twist and the rear legs will align, and then the cat will arch its back to lessen the impact of the landing.

The most popular names for female cats in the USA are: Missy, Misty, Muffin, Patches, Fluffy, Tabitha, Tigger, Pumpkin and Samantha.

A Hippopotamus can run faster than you.

A Kangaroo can jump only if its tail is touching the ground.

A newborn turkey chick has to be taught to eat, or it will starve.

In their entire lifetime, twelve average worker bees will produce only one teaspoonful of honey.

A plug socket in Britain supplies 240 volts.
The average Electric Eel discharge is more
than 350 volts, but discharges as high as 650
volts have been measured.

Pigs are often thought to be dirty, but actually keep themselves cleaner than most pets. They are seen lying in mud because they do not have sweat glands and constantly need water or mud to cool off.

Elephants have 24 teeth. The teeth do not grow all at once, but in fours. As the first set wears down, a second set grows. At the age of 45 an elephant grows its last teeth, each weighing 4 kg (9lb).

The easiest way to tell if an animal is a carnivore or a vegetarian is by looking at the positioning of its eyes. Hunting animals have eyes located in the front of their heads, so they can focus in on the prey that they are stalking. Vegetarian animals have eyes on the side of their heads so they can see the hunters coming at them from all directions.

The domestic cat is the only cat species able to hold its tail vertically while walking. All wild cats hold their tails horizontally or tucked between their legs while walking.

Dolphins swim in circles while they sleep with the eye on the outside of the circle open to keep watch for predators. After a certain amount of time, they turn round and swim in the opposite direction with the opposite eye open.

Crocodiles kill 2,000 people each year.

A large ostrich running at speed will take steps over twenty-five feet long.

Kermit the Frog is left-handed.

Some moths never eat anything as adults because they don't have mouths. They live on the energy they stored up as caterpillars.

Panda bears are not really bears.

Mentioning pigs is bad luck at sea.

Dogs get 18 mentions in the Bible, cats none.

Judge Turtle, of the California Supreme Court, awarded 3,500 dollars damages to a seven-year-old elephant which lost its talent for water-skiing after a road accident.

New insect species are discovered at the rate of nearly a thousand a year.

The Kiwi, national bird of New Zealand, can't fly. It lives in a hole in the ground, is almost completely blind, and lays only one egg each year. Despite all this, it has survived on Earth for more than 70 million years.

A hippo can open its mouth so wide that a
four-foot-tall person could walk in.

The world's first guide dog was an Alsatian bred by a wealthy American woman in Switzerland in the 1920s. Buddy was sent to America where she became a "Seeing Eye Dog" for her lucky new owner, Morris Frank.

It is possible that whales can hear each other a hundred miles apart.

Owls have eyesight over a hundred times better than ours.

Technically, a starfish just a little bag of nerves.

A crocodile's digestive juices are so strong that it can digest a steel nail.

Silkworm larvae will eat a tonne of mulberry leaves to make five kilograms of silk.

The Cicada, an insect found in Africa, spends 17 years of its life sleeping; it wakes up for just two weeks during which it mates and then dies.

A whale can swim for 3 months without eating.

Turtles can live for more than 100 years.

Termite queens are bigger than the normal ones and can lay up to 30,000 eggs in a single day.

Kangaroo Rats never drink. They absorb fluids from the food they eat and air they breathe.

If a Tarantula loses a leg in a fight, it will more than likely grow it back again.

The Patu Marplesi Spider from Western Samoa is less than half a millimetre in width.

The toughest insects on Earth are probably Springtails, found in Antarctica. They are happy in temperatures below -50 Centigrade and can live without oxygen for up to a month. The clever little chaps actually produce their own anti-freeze to stop them getting chilly.

The word peacock actually refers to the male bird, while females are peahens, and the young are peachicks.

Killer Whales are voluntary breathers. That means they have to sleep with only half of their brain at one time. The other half has to stay awake to remember to breathe.

Cats have over 100 vocal sounds, while dogs have only about ten.

The Cheetah can accelerate to 45 miles per hour in just two seconds.

Frogs must close their eyes to swallow.

The cat, the camel and the giraffe are rare among four-footed creatures because they move both left legs followed by both right legs when they walk. Almost all other mammals alternate the legs.

If a cow steps on your foot, and you can keep your calm, simply lean forward into the cow and it will move away.

Did you know...

...that the Goliath Beetle can carry up to 850 times its own weight?

What's the origin of the word "barbecue?" It came from French-speaking pirates, who enjoyed a Caribbean pork feast called "de barbe à queue," which translates as "from beard to tail." In other words, they ate the whole pig.

The male Gypsy Moth can smell the female Gypsy Moth from two miles away.

Walt Disney's Goofy started life with the name Dippy Dawg before he met Mickey Mouse and never looked back.

Sharks have fantastic eyesight, great night vision and they can distinguish colours. Yellow, white, and silver seem to attract them. Divers should pick dark colours for swimming with sharks.

Elephants get by on only two hours of sleep a day.

Heavy rock music makes termites chew through wood at twice their usual speed.

The oldest cow ever recorded was an Irish Dremon named Big Bertha. She was nearly 49 when she died.

An elephant can be pregnant for up to 22 months.

The ancestor of all domestic cats is the African Wild Cat, which still exists today.

Dog saliva is cleaner than a human's.

There are pink dolphins in the Amazon river.

The only place in Europe where monkeys live free is Gibraltar.

You can tell the sex of a turtle by the sound it makes. A male grunts: a female hisses.

Before a Tarantula bites you, it will stand on its back legs baring its little fangs. The bites are poisonous, but most breeds do no more damage than your average bee sting.

Even though cockroaches have been on the Earth for 250,000,000 years, they have not changed at all.

Honeybees have hair on their eyes.

A cow's sweat glands are in her nose.

Cats have two sets of vocal chords.

A baboon called "Jackie" became a private in the South African army in World War I.

Tuna can swim at speeds up to 50 miles per hour in short bursts.

Turkey Vultures are able to pick up the smell of carrion (the meat of dead animals) from over a mile away.

About 18 per cent of animal owners share their bed with their pet.

A single sheep's fleece might well contain as many as 26 million hairs.

A square mile of fertile earth has about 32,000,000 Earthworms in it.

A Woodchuck usually breathes 2,100 times an hour, but it breathes only ten times an hour while it is hibernating.

At birth, a Panda is smaller than a mouse and weighs about four ounces.

Australia has the largest sheep population.

Bats always turn left when exiting a cave.

Carnivorous animals will not eat another animal that has been hit by lightning.

Woodpecker scalps, porpoise teeth, and giraffe tails have all been used as money.

The fingerprints of Koala Bears are virtually indistinguishable from those of humans, so much so that they could be confused at a crime scene.

Snails produce a sticky slime that forms a protective carpet under them as they travel along. The slime is so effective that they can crawl along the edge of a razor blade without hurting themselves.

Snakes are immune to their own poison.

Some baby Giraffes are more than six feet tall at birth.

Greyhounds have the best eyesight of any breed of dog.

A greyhound can reach speeds of up to 42 miles per hour.

A single pig gave birth to 34 piglets in Denmark in 1961.

Worker ants may live seven years and the queen may live as long as 15 years.

An Octopus will eat its own arms if it gets really hungry.

To escape the grip of a crocodile's jaws, push your thumbs into its eyeballs - it will let you go.

Owls are the only animals that can turn their heads a full 180 degrees.

The Blue Whale weighs forty tons more than the largest dinosaur ever discovered.

Chickens that lay brown eggs have red ear lobes: there is a genetic link between the two things.

Rabbits love licorice.

Pet parrots can eat virtually any common food eaten by humans except for chocolate and avocados. Both of these are highly toxic to the parrot and can be fatal.

Koalas never drink water. They get fluids from the eucalyptus leaves they eat.

Male lions can sleep for up to 20 hours a day.

The female lion does more than 90 per cent of the hunting while the male prefers to rest.

A rodent's teeth never stop growing. They are worn down by the animal's constant gnawing on bark, leaves, and other vegetation.

Caterpillars have about 4,000 muscles. Humans, by comparison, have only about 600.

Goldfish lose their colour if they are kept in dim light or are placed in a body of running water, such as a stream.

It was discovered on a space mission that a frog can throw up. The frog throws up its stomach first, so the stomach is dangling out of its mouth. Then the frog uses its forearms to dig out all of the stomach's contents and then swallows the stomach back down again.

If monkeys eat too many unripe bananas, their tongue and eyes will turn green.

Did you know...

...that contrary to their carnivorous image, Grizzly Bears are primarily vegetarians?

By feeding hens certain dyes they can be made to lay eggs with different coloured yolks.

Every year in America, $1.5 billion is spent on pet food. This is four times the amount spent on baby food.

The penalty for killing a cat, 4,000 years ago in Egypt, was death.

Polar bears are so well insulated they tend to overheat.

King Louis XI of France once commanded one of his abbots to invent a new and ridiculous musical instrument for the amusement of the Court. The abbot gathered together a series of pigs, each with their own distinctive squeal, and proceeded to prod each one of them in turn to provide a tune.

Herons have been observed dropping insects on water and then catching the fish that come up to eat them.

The flea can jump 350 times its body length. That's like a human jumping the length of a football field.

Alsatians bite humans more than any other breed of dog.

Cats wag their tails when they are deciding something. Once the cat makes a decision, the tail will immediately stop wagging.

There can be more insects in one square mile of rural land than there are human beings on the entire earth.

African Heart-nosed Bats can hear the footsteps of a beetle walking on sand from a distance of more than six feet.

Charles II first tried dog racing in 1670 at Hampton Court Palace. It wasn't until 250 years later that racing greyhounds took off as a popular sport, largely due to the invention of the mechanical hare. Early hares were mounted on roller skates and pulled along with string.

A dragonfly has a lifespan of 24 hours.

Elephants spend approximately 75% of their day eating.

The Goliath Bird-eating Spider from South America can grow to 300 mm across and live for nearly 30 years.

The biggest butterfly in the world is the Queen Alexandra's Birdwing from Papua New Guinea. At 280 mm across, it's as big as a dinner plate.

Elephants can communicate using sounds so deep, humans can't hear them.

The cells which make up the antlers of a moose are the fastest-growing animal cells in nature.

Bats can't walk: their legs are too thin.

The only female animal that has antlers is the caribou.

Butterflies were originally called flutterbies.

The Arctic Giant Jellyfish's tentacles have been known to grow up to 36.5 metres (120 feet) long.

Some centipedes really do have 100 legs. However, the most legs a Pill Millipede will ever have is 38.

When angered, the Tasmanian Devil turns a pinkish-red.

Kangaroos need very little water to survive and are capable of going for months without drinking at all. When they do need water, they dig wells for themselves, frequently going as deep as three or four feet. These 'kangaroo pits' are a handy source of water for other animals.

Giraffes have no vocal cords.

The Black Bear and the Chow dog both have blue tongues.

Ostriches produce the strongest leather you can buy.

Ants don't sleep.

A goldfish has a memory span of about three seconds.

An ostrich's eye is bigger than its brain.

In China the Man in the Moon is a toad.

Of the 4,000 species of mammals on the planet, 900 of them are bats.

The word alligator comes from "El Lagarto" which is Spanish for "The Lizard."

Lobsters grow by moulting. This is the process in which they climb out of their old shells and grow a new one. This moulting, or shell-shedding, occurs about 25-30 times in a young lobster's life, and once a year when they are adult. When they have struggled out of the old shell, the lobster eats everything in sight in order to grow, including the old shell.

A cat in Japan says "neow".

A cat in Thailand says "mao".

A cow in Thailand says "oo-ah".

A dog in Bangkok says "bahk-bahk".

A dog in Japan says "wan-wan".

A dog in East Africa says "woo-woo".

A rooster in Germany says "ay-ee-ache-ache".

A scorpion could survive for three weeks if it was embedded in a block of ice.

A stingray never actually sees the food as it eats, since its eyes are on top of its head and its mouth and nostrils are on the bottom.

A dog can suffer from tonsillitis, but not appendicitis. They don't have an appendix.

A shark can detect one part of blood in 100 million parts of water.

The loudest sound ever recorded from an animal was produced by a Blue Whale.

The gene for the Siamese coloration in cats is heat sensitive. Warmth produces a lighter colour than does cold. Putting tape temporarily on a Siamese cat's ear will make the fur on that ear lighter than on the other ear.

Ninety per cent of all species that have become extinct have been birds.

Sharks can go for over a year without eating.

Earth's chickens lay 400 billion eggs a year.

The Leatherback is the largest sea turtle. Individuals have reached a shell length of 1.85 metres (6 feet) and weights of 637 kilograms (1,400 pounds); they eat mainly jellyfish.

The largest lizard in the world is the Komodo Dragon, named because of its fire-coloured tongue. It can grow longer than a car.

The Hummingbird, the Loon, the Swift, the Kingfisher, and the Grebe are all birds that cannot walk.

A cat's heart beats twice as fast as a human heart, at 110 to 140 beats per minute.

If your cat is near you, and its tail is quivering, this is the greatest expression of affection a cat can give.

A dog can't hear the lowest note on a piano.

Squirrels have been known to lick the salt off roads that have been de-iced.

In Brooklyn, N.Y., it's illegal to let a dog sleep in your bath.

Seven elephants and dancing bears survived the sinking of the Titanic and got jobs in New York afterwards.

Did you know...

...that a mole can dig a tunnel over three hundred feet long in a single night?

An elephant can smell water three miles away.

Cat whiskers can detect movements 2,000 times smaller than the width of a human hair.

Werewolves, or lycanthropes, as they are also known, are people who assume the form of a wolf during a full moon. They then catch people and eat them up, the younger the better.

How to spot a werewolf.
1. They are very hairy, even on the palms of their hands.
2. Their eyebrows often meet in the centre of their foreheads.
3. They wear a pice of wolfskin, usually as a belt or bracelet.
4. They have pointed ears.

Parrots rarely acquire a vocabulary of more than 20 words. However, Tymhoney Greys and African Greys have been know to learn and speak in excess of 100 words.

Emperor Penguins can catch and kill a squid measuring up to three feet long.

A single Little Brown Bat can eat up to 1,000 mosquitoes in a single hour.

A camel can narrow or clamp its nostrils tightly shut when it needs to. Special muscles keep much of the dust and blowing sand from getting sucked into its nose.

A single pair of cats and their kittens can produce as many as 420,000 more kittens in just seven years.

Most tropical marine fish could survive in a tank filled with human blood.

The raccoon derives its name from the Indian word meaning "he who scratches with his hands".

Ostrich racing is a popular sport in South Africa.

The females of some moth species lack wings. All they can do to move is crawl.

Les King claimed a unique "fish-in-one" in September 1983 when a drive from the 17th tee on his golf course in Norfolk flew into a nearby river and stunned a two-foot-long Pike.

The sweat glands of a squirrel are in its feet.

Chameleons can move one eye in a different direction from the other eye.

A skunk's smell can be detected by a human a mile away.

The foot is the most common body part bitten by insects.

The Catfish has the most taste buds of all animals, having over 27,000 of them.

The snail mates only once in its entire life.

A lion in the wild usually makes no more than 20 kills a year.

It's against the law to have a pet in Iceland.

Scorpions can withstand 200 times more nuclear radiation than humans can.

Cats can sense the chlorine or other minerals in tap water. Some won't drink it.

The Sooty Tern can remain on the wing for as long as three years before it returns to its nesting ground.

Tigers have striped
skin, not just
striped fur.

The dog family (Canids) includes the Wolf, Fox, Coyote, Jackal and Australian Dingo. They live everywhere from the frozen ice floes of the North (Arctic Fox) to the Sahara Desert (the tiny Fennec).

Mosquitoes prefer biting children to adults, and blondes to brunettes.

When a queen bee lays the fertilised eggs that will develop into new queens, only one of the newly laid queens actually survives. The first new queen that emerges from her cell destroys all other queens in their cells and, thereafter, reigns alone.

Donald Duck's middle name is Fauntleroy.

Fish do not have eyelids and therefore cannot blink. Blinking spreads moisture over the surface of the eye, and since fish live in water they don't need to do this.

Salmon have a lot of offspring, generally from 2,500 to 7,000 depending on the species and size of fish. The Chinook Salmon generally produces the most and largest eggs.

When Bugs Bunny first appeared in 1935, he was called Happy Rabbit.

Cats spend 16 hours of each day sleeping.

Gibbons can swing from tree to tree at speeds of up to 35 mph, 200 feet above the ground.

Bats are more closely related to humans than they are to rodents.

The female Knot-tying Weaverbird will refuse to mate with a male who has built a shoddy nest. If he is turned down, the male must take the nest apart and completely rebuild it in order to win the affections of the female.

A cat is more inclined to watch TV than a dog is, according to experts.

Calling a puppy to punish it teaches the dog not to come when it's called. It's best to reward your dog by bringing it to you, and to punish it by sending it away.

Some apes in the wild have been observed whistling.

A hummingbird has a larger heart for its size than any other bird. Such a big motor needs a lot of fuel, so a hummingbird has to eat 50 or 60 meals every day. If its heartbeat did not slow down, and its body temperature drop several degrees at night, it would starve to death while sleeping.

A Blue Whale's heart beats only nine times per minute.

A cat uses its whiskers to work out if a space is too small to squeeze through.

A shark can grow a new set of teeth in a week. When sharks bite, their eyes roll back and their teeth protrude from their heads.

On average, city dogs live longer than country dogs: 11 years as compared to 8. Some breeds can live up to 25 years old and beyond.

Did you know...

...that unlike Lions, Tigers and Panthers, Cheetahs are unable to roar?

The Mantis shrimp catches its prey by stunning it with a sudden chop from its claws. This force is so massive that Mantis shrimps can't be kept in aquariums, because they can easily smash the glass of the tank. Their claws are among the fastest-moving animal parts known on Earth. The impact of a Mantis claw blow is as powerful as a bullet fired from a gun.

The fastest bird is probably the Spine-tailed Swift, clocked flying at speeds of up to 220 miles per hour.

Goldfish are photosensitive. Their skin colour reacts to sunlight.

A squirrel will clean a nut by licking it or rubbing it on its face before it is buried. This action applies a scent to the nut which helps the squirrel find it later, even under a foot of snow.

Camels chew in a figure-of-eight pattern.

Sailfish can leap out of the water and into the air at a speed of 50 miles (81 km) per hour.

The cockroach's favourite food is the glue on the back of stamps.

Tuna swim at a steady rate of nine miles per hour until they die and they never stop moving. That means that by the time a tuna reaches 15 years old, it will have swum more than one million miles.

An adult hippo can bite a twelve-foot adult male crocodile in half.

At full speed, a Cheetah takes strides 26 feet (8 m) long.

The fastest moving land snail, the Common Garden Snail, has a speed of 0.0313 mph.

The phrase "raining cats and dogs" originated in 17th-century England. During heavy downpours the roads flooded and many of these poor animals unfortunately drowned. Their bodies would be seen floating in the torrents that ran through the streets. This gave the appearance that it had actually rained "cats and dogs" and led to the expression.

Camel humps are not storage places for water, but for fat.

A cat will amost never "meow" at another cat. This sound is reserved for humans.

The hippo's yawn is not a sign of sleepiness or boredom but is actually a threat gesture, displaying long, thick, razor-sharp teeth, with which it is capable of biting a small boat clean in two.

The zoo in Tokyo closes for two months of the year so the animals can have a holiday from the visitors.

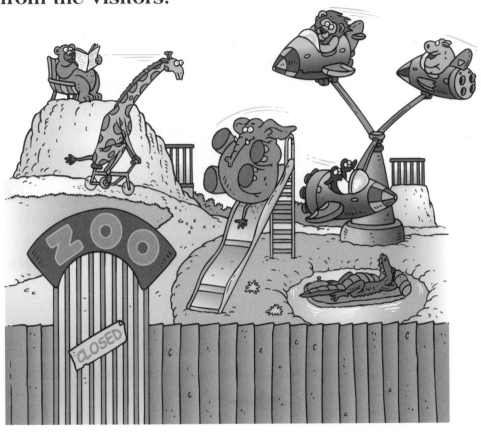

Police in Seville, Spain reported in the autumn of 1983 that an Alsatian dog, trained by a criminal, was snatching handbags in the city streets.

Most cats prefer their food at room temperature, rather than from the fridge.

Cats need five times more protein in their diet than dogs do.

The Alaskan King Crab is the largest of the crustaceans, weighing up to 15 pounds, and measuring four to five feet across shell and claws.

The last Dodo bird died in 1681.

Butterflies cannot fly if their body temperature is less than 86 degrees.

Dry fish food can make goldfish constipated.

In Nairobi, Kenya, leopards steal food right from people's dustbins. Let's face it, who's going to tell them to stop?

Gibbons can project their voices up to two miles through dense rainforest.

A beaver can gnaw through a log the thickness of a rolling pin in 30 seconds.

Sir Isaac Newton, discoverer of the scientific principles of gravity, also invented the cat flap.

A mole could tunnel under a football pitch lengthwise in a single day.

Scallops are jet-propelled. The sea creature compresses the valves of its shell and forces water backward in jets near the shell hinge. The force drives the scallop along in the direction of the shell opening.

A maverick is a cow that escaped getting branded.

Sharks do not have bones. They are made up of cartilage. This makes it hard for scientists to study ancient sharks, because cartilage, unlike bones, doesn't form fossils. The only remains from million-year-old sharks from the past are their teeth.

Cats spend 30% of their waking hours grooming themselves.

The word "gazelle" comes from the Arabian term for affectionate, and is believed to be inspired by the creature's large, gentle eyes.

Some midges beat their wings at up to 62,760 times a minute. Not surprisingly, they don't live very long.

A geep is a cross between a goat and a sheep.

The biggest pig in recorded history was Big Boy of Black Mountain, North Carolina, who weighed 1,904 pounds in 1939.

A cat has five more vertebrae in its spinal column than a human does.

Ancient Egyptians kept dogs for their looks as well as for hunting. Vases depicting the beautiful Afghan Hound have been unearthed that date back to 4000 BC.

Macaroni, Gentoo, Chinstrap and Emperor are all types of penguins.

The most valuable fish ever caught was a Russian sturgeon caught in 1924. The eggs of the sturgeon are a much prized dish called caviar, eaten in the world's poshest restaurants. Inside this sturgeon was 540 pounds of the stuff, worth a princely £200,000.

The world's biggest bat is the massive Flying Fox of southern Asia, with a wingspan of 1.7 metres. The smallest is the tiny Hog-Nosed Bat of south-western Thailand, which is about the size of a Bumble Bee. In San Antonio, Texas, the Bracken Cave is the world's most batty, with over 20 million squeaky inhabitants.

Owls have eyeballs that are tubular in shape. Because of this, they can't move their eyes.

Did you know...

...that shrews eat more than their own bodyweight in food every day?

The oldest fish ever was a female European eel called Putte, who lived in the Halsingborg museum in Sweden to the ripe old age of 88.

A baby eel is called an elver; a baby oyster is called a spat.

The term "Three dog night" for a chilly evening (attributed to Australian Aborigines) came about because on especially cold nights these nomadic people needed three dogs to sleep with to keep from freezing.

Lobsters can live for a hundred years.

Dogs are more likely to bite a stranger that runs than one that doesn't move.

Newborn hedgehogs are born with their spines just below the skin. Spines start to appear outwardly within 24 hours of birth.

The Bald Eagle is not really bald; it actually has white feathers on its head, neck, and tail. Bald is a derivation of "balde", an Old English word meaning white. The Bald Eagle was named because of its white feathers rather than a lack of them.

Bald Eagles can actually swim. They use an overhand movement of the wings that is very much like the butterfly stroke.

A raven could take the laces out of your shoes with its beak.

Bottlenose Dolphins generally do not need to dive very deeply to catch food. Depending on habitat, most Bottlenose Dolphins regularly dive to depths of 3 to 45.7 metres (10-150 feet). They are, however, capable of diving to greater depths. Under experimental conditions, a trained dolphin has reached a depth of 547 metres.

The colour of a kitten's eyes will change as it grows older.

The word puppy comes from the French poupée, meaning "doll".

The female ants are ones that do all the work.

Ants keep slaves. Certain species raid the nests of other ants, kill the queen, and kidnap many of the workers. The workers are brought back to the captors' nest and forced into performing menial tasks.

The jaws of African Fire Ants are used as stitches for wounds in Kenya. After an operation is performed, an ant is allowed to bite into the skin along either side of the incision. The ant's body is then twisted off, leaving the head with its teeth locked into the skin like a stitch.

A pig in Russia says "ha-roo".
A pig in Thailand says "oot-oot".
A pig in Japan says "moo-moo".

The largest cat breed is the Ragdoll. Males weigh twelve to twenty pounds, with females weighing ten to fifteen pounds. The smallest cat breed is the Singapura. Males weigh about six pounds while females weigh about four pounds.

Walruses have an inventive way of uncovering their food. They take in a big mouthful of water and squirt it at the sand on the ocean floor. This moves the sand out of the way exposing a tasty morsel like a clam or a worm.

Blue Whales have weighed up to 146 metric tonnes (160 tons).

In the old days, sea captains kept pigs on board ship because they believed, should they be shipwrecked, that the pigs would always swim toward the nearest shore. This isn't necessarily true.

Warthogs always reverse into their burrows. This enables them to defend themselves. In the mornings, Warthogs burst out of their burrows at top speed to get a running start on any predators that may be lurking nearby.

Even though a Carpet Python is not warm-blooded, a female can raise her body temperature by twitching her muscles. This muscular activity creates enough warmth for her to incubate the eggs.

There are approximately 80 teeth in an alligator's mouth at any time. When they wear down they are replaced and the alligator can go through 2,000 or 3,000 teeth in a lifetime.

Orangutans shelter themselves from rain and sun by holding leafy branches over their heads, and when constructing a night nest in the trees, will sometimes add a leafy roof.

100 years ago, 20 tons of ivory were shipped every year from Siberia to London, all taken from the remains of Woolly Mammoths, which have been extinct since the Ice Age.

Only female bees work. Males remain in the hive and literally do nothing, their only mission in life being to fertilise the queen bee on her maiden flight. For this purpose literally thousands of males are hatched, out of which only one or two mate with the queen. After they have served their function, the males are not allowed back into the hive but are left outside, where they starve to death.

Swinging through the trees, hanging like a monkey does, is called "brachiating".

The heaviest pile of elephant droppings recorded weighed 300 pounds.

The fastest insect on the ground is a cockroach, clocking in at 5.4 kph. The human equivalent would be running 100 metres in one second.

Aardvark means "earth pig" in the Afrikaans language, due to their long heads and large ears. Their ant-catching tongue is sticky and can reach 18 inches from the mouth.

Within an hour of birth, a Zebra foal can run with the rest of the herd and can recognize its mother by smell and sight.

The most athletic insect must be the flea. They can jump up to 130 times their own height. A person that springy could hurdle the Eiffel Tower easily.

Walruses in the water are dark grey in colour, but when one has been sunbathing for any length of time, it turns pink.

A scorpion can remain pregnant for 18 months before giving birth. That's twice as long as the human gestation period.

Newly hatched flamingos are covered with soft grey feathers. The chicks acquire their bubblegum pink plumage as they approach their third birthday.

Sacred Ibis birds live in large colonies near rivers throughout Africa. In ancient Egyptian societies, the Sacred Ibis was worshipped as a god. The birds were often mummified, then buried with pharaohs.

People who live in Topeka, Kansas, and own more than five cats, are breaking the law.

Marabou Storks are attracted to grass fires. They march in front of the advancing flames grabbing animals that are fleeing.

Caligula, the Roman Emperor from A.D. 37 to 41, appointed his favourite horse as consul and co-regent of Rome. He was generally considered to be mad.

African Black-footed Penguins, although they cannot fly, can swim at up to 25 miles per hour. That's faster than a Bottlenose Dolphin.

A South African monkey was promoted to the rank of corporal during World War I.

An Armadillo crosses a river by holding its breath and walking across the bottom.

Guinea pigs are put in with rabbits by farmers because they serve as guards against rat attacks. The Guineas sense a rat approaching and let out a very loud scream which frightens the rats away.

When a homing pigeon was released from Pembrokeshire, England in June 1953, it was expected to return home that night. Instead it returned, dead, by post eleven years later postmarked "Brazil".

The British racehorse "Humourist", who won the English Derby in the early 1920's, should never have been able to race. When he died shortly after the Derby, it was discovered that he had been born with only one lung.

The reason fire stations have spiral stairways dates back to when engines were pulled by horses. The horses were kept on the ground floor and worked out how to climb straight staircases.

Did you know…

…that Arctic Squirrels hibernate for nine months of the year?

In American farm terminology, a pig becomes a hog when it reaches 100 pounds in weight.

All domestic cats hate lemons.

In France, they used to sell rabbits skinned, but with their feet still attached. The reason being it is very difficult to tell a skinned cat from a skinned rabbit without the feet.

Rabbits can be litterbox trained like cats.

If monkeys eat too many unripe bananas their tongues will turn green.

Never squash a Yellowjacket Wasp. A dying Yellowjacket releases a smell that alerts its comrades. In less than 15 seconds, Yellowjackets within a 15-foot radius will come to help out their friend.

If you enjoyed this book, you can find more hilarious jokes, amazing facts, and brainbusting riddles and puzzles in the following books, also published by Dean:

Title	ISBN
The World's Funniest Animal Jokes for Kids	0 603 56064 4
The World's Funniest Disgusting Jokes for Kids	0 603 56065 2
The World's Funniest School Jokes for Kids	0 603 56063 6
The World's Most Amazing Planet Earth Facts for Kids	0 603 56062 8
The World's Most Amazing Science Facts for Kids	0 603 56061X
1000 of the World's Funniest Jokes for Kids	0 603 56066 0
1000 of the World's Most Astonishing Facts for Kids	0 603 56067 9
1000 of the World's Greatest Brainbusters	0 603 56068 7